STRONG BONDS!

The Chemistry of **Building Materials**

Written by William D. Adams

www.worldbook.com

Co-published by agreement between Shi Tu Hui and World Book, Inc.

Shi Tu Hui
Room 1807, Block 1,
#3 West Dawang Road
Chaoyang District, Beijing 100025
P.R. China

World Book, Inc.
180 North LaSalle Street
Suite 900
Chicago, Illinois 60601
USA

© 2026. All rights reserved. This volume may not be reproduced in whole or in part in any form without prior written permission from the publisher.

WORLD BOOK and the GLOBE DEVICE are registered trademarks or trademarks of World Book, Inc.

Library of Congress Control Number: 2025942239

Aha! Academy: Chemistry
ISBN: 978-0-7166-7346-0 (set, hardcover)

Strong Bonds! The Chemistry of Building Materials
ISBN: 978-0-7166-7352-1 (hard cover)
ISBN: 978-0-7166-7372-9 (e-book)
ISBN: 978-0-7166-7362-0 (soft cover)

Staff

Editorial

Vice President
Tom Evans

Senior Manager, New Content
Jeff De La Rosa

Senior Curriculum Designer
Caroline Davidson

Curriculum Designer
Mikayla Kightlinger

Content Creator
Joseph P. Cataliotti

Proofreader
Nathalie Strassheim

Indexer
Nathaniel Lindstrom

Graphics and Design

Senior Visual
Communications Designer
Melanie Bender

Designer
Shannon Hagman

Written by William D. Adams

Designed by Starletta Polster

Acknowledgments

The publishers gratefully acknowledge the following sources for photography. All illustrations were prepared by WORLD BOOK unless otherwise noted.

Cover: Chonlatee42/Shutterstock; DedMityay/Shutterstock; Irene Miller/Shutterstock; Maksim Safaniuk/Shutterstock; Singha Songsak P/Shutterstock

© B.O'Kane/Alamy 23; © Eden Breitz/Alamy 29; © D and S Photography Archives/Alamy 34; © GL Archive/Alamy 17; © history_docu_photo/Alamy 35; © NASA Image Collection/Alamy 33; © Niday Picture Library/Alamy 9; © Pictorial Press Ltd/Alamy 36; © Photo Recall/Alamy 15; © The Syndicate/Alamy 41; © World History Archive/Alamy 36; Public Domain 15; © Shutterstock 3, 4, 5, 6, 7, 8, 9, 10, 11, 12, 13, 14, 15, 16, 17, 18, 19, 20, 21, 22, 23, 24, 25, 26, 27, 28, 29, 30, 31, 32, 33, 34, 35, 36, 37, 38, 39, 40, 41, 42, 43, 44, 45, 46, 47, 48

There is a glossary of terms on page 48. Terms defined in the glossary are in type that looks like *this* on their first appearance on any spread (two facing pages).

Contents

Introduction 4

① **The house that chemistry built** 6

　We're good with wood 8
　The future of wood 10
　Vital element: iron 12
　Strong steel 14
　Rust busts steel 16
　Concrete strength 18
　Uses for concrete 20
　Another brick in the wall .22
　Mudbricks 24
　Let the sunshine in 26
　Roofing 28

② **Inside the home** 30

　Staying warm with insulation 32
　Asbestos: deadly rock fibers 34
　Vital element: argon 36
　Drywall 38
　Household paint chemistry 40
　Chemistry will floor you! .42

Material strength 44
Index 46
Glossary 48

Introduction

Odds are that you're reading this book inside a building. Think of all the materials needed to build it. Those materials were created using chemistry and derive their strength from it. It's true! Everything makes use of chemistry—even buildings!

Humans have been living in structures for many thousands of years. As we've discovered more about technology, our buildings have evolved from homely hovels to soaring steel skyscrapers.

Sometimes, steel skyscrapers aren't all they're cracked up to be—and homely hovels are more desirable! Materials scientists and engineers have looked to materials of the past and reimagined the materials of the present. The buildings of tomorrow may be taller, stronger, and more energy efficient—all thanks to chemistry!

1

THE HOUSE THAT CHEMISTRY BUILT

Every building on Earth is the house that chemistry built! The strength of a building material comes from its chemistry.

How does a skyscraper stand up

or a single-family home withstand strong winds? What makes a modern office resistant to fire? The answers lie in the chemistry of the materials that make up the building. The chemical makeup of a material plays a major part in its physical properties, such as how hard it is or how much it can bend. Based on those properties, we select different materials for different purposes. Builders use many kinds of materials to build a structure. A knowledge of chemistry can help select a material right for each job.

CAREER CORNER

Who designs houses, skyscrapers, and everything in between? Architects! An architect is a person who designs and lays out plans for buildings. But, you won't find an architect at the job site swinging a hammer! Instead, their plans are carried out by the contractors and workers who actually put up the building. Architects must balance many different factors when designing a building, taking into account the client's demands, energy efficiency, building strength, and aesthetic choices.

The house that chemistry built

We're good with wood

Wood consists of tiny, tube-shaped cells that form layers of permanent tissue around a plant stem. The walls of wood cells are made of three chief substances—cellulose, lignin, and hemicellulose. Cellulose makes up about half of wood by weight. It is soft and consists of fibers. Lignin, on the other hand, is a heavy, solid material that is found between strands of cellulose and between the wood cells themselves. Lignin makes wood hard and stiff. Hemicellulose helps to hold cellulose strands together. Wood also contains substances called *extractives*. They include fats, gums, oils, and coloring matter.

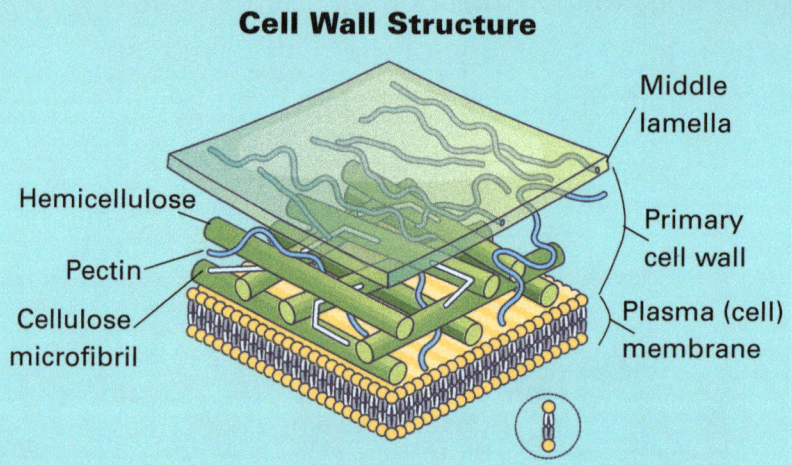

Cell Wall Structure

Wood's chemical makeup gives it great physical properties for building. It's strong, particularly in the direction of its grain—that's the length of the trunk—enabling builders to make strong posts. Despite its strength, it's surprisingly easy to work! Wood can be cut into different sizes, drilled with holes to allow for fittings, and held together with nails and screws. Is there anything wood can't do?

How about a construction material that's so common it literally grows on trees! Wood has been prized for tens of thousands of years for its strength, workability, and beauty.

Despite being dead, wood is uniquely resistant to decay—as long as it stays dry. Wood is naturally quite dry, and lumber is dried in large ovens to remove as much moisture as possible. Cellulose and lignin form a barrier against water and microbes that might break down the wood. But if the moisture content reaches 20 percent or higher, fungi will start to grow and digest the wood. Special care must be taken when wood is used in moist environments or touching the ground, where it can pick up moisture.

> We'd eat your house, but it's too dry!

Lumber has one great weakness as a building material: its susceptibility to fire. Wood burns in **combustion**, a chemical reaction in which oxygen combines with carbon-based fuel to produce carbon dioxide, water vapor, and heat. For centuries, fires were the bane of densely populated cities with wood-framed buildings. London, Chicago, Boston—famous fires swept through these cities, causing massive damage and loss of life. Such fires led many densely packed cities to turn away from wood in favor of more fire-resistant building materials.

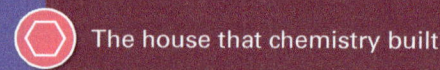
The house that chemistry built

The future of wood

In many places, particularly in the United States, builders have gotten good at making small buildings fast, using a minimum of wood. Platform construction makes use of small, narrow pieces of lumber to quickly build walls. A skilled crew can frame up a new home in a matter of days. But platform framing is only feasible in smaller, low-lying buildings, such as single-family homes or small apartment complexes.

I'm the Wooden Wonder!

Wood got new life with the invention of epoxy resins in the early 1940's. These resins are long-chain molecules that start out as a viscous liquid but set when exposed to air or heat, making the wood strong and extremely water-resistant. The British airplane manufacturer De Havilland used these epoxies to assemble *Mosquito* fighter bombers, which were used in World War II (1939-1945).

The strength and environmental friendliness of wood are leading architects and engineers of large buildings to give this material another look.

Architects have designed large structures, including skyscrapers, out of a wood material called **mass timber**.

The danger of fire remains, however. Proponents of mass timber point out that, in some ways, the material outperforms steel in a fire. Wood surfaces char when exposed to fire, which can protect the material underneath. But unlike steel, mass timber is flammable. Use of the material in larger buildings will likely require flame-resistant coatings and advanced sprinkler systems.

TECH TIME

Mass timber is a group of wood products created by bonding timbers together with adhesives, dowels, nails, or screws. The bonding of multiple planks gives mass timber building elements strength in multiple directions. Huge sections of mass timber can be used in place of steel beams or prefabricated concrete walls.

The house that chemistry built

Vital element: iron

STATS

Symbol
Fe

Atomic Number
26

Atomic Mass
55.845

Melting Point
2795 °F (1535 °C)

Boiling Point
5100 °F (2800 °C)

Iron atoms join with one another through metallic bonding. In metallic bonding, each nucleus shares its electrons among all its neighbors. Other elements can easily get mixed in if they are present when the molten metal cools to a solid. A mixture of a metal and at least one other element is called an *alloy*.

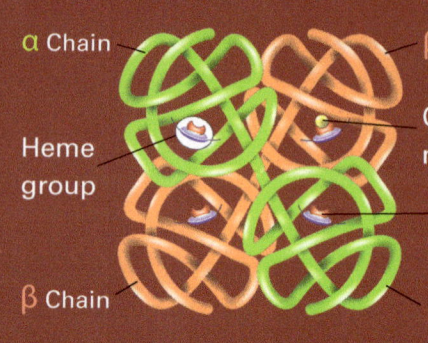

Hemoglobin
- α Chain
- β Chain
- Heme group
- Oxygen molecule
- Iron
- β Chain
- α Chain

Iron is the main element in *hemoglobin*, the *molecule* that transports oxygen in the blood. In the lungs, oxygen bonds to the iron in hemoglobin. In the body, hemoglobin releases the oxygen and bonds to carbon dioxide.

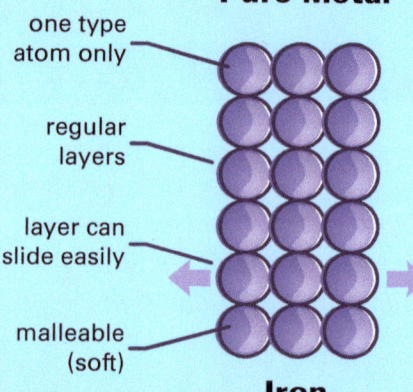

Pure Metal — Iron
- one type atom only
- regular layers
- layer can slide easily
- malleable (soft)

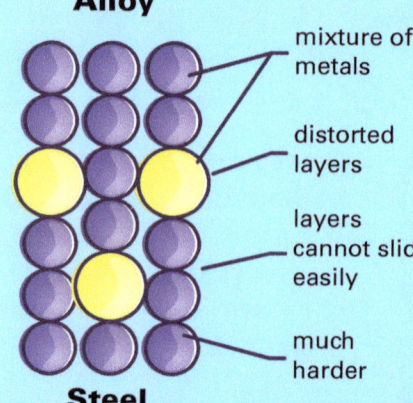

Alloy — Steel
- mixture of metals
- distorted layers
- layers cannot slide easily
- much harder

12

Iron is the most abundant metal

on Earth and the most useful metal to people and other living things. It's in our buildings, ball bearings, and blood.

Making an alloy is kind of like baking! Much as a finished cake has a different taste than its raw ingredients (yuck!), an alloy has different properties than its elemental components. Also as in baking, the recipe matters. An alloy with 10 percent of one element might have different physical properties than an alloy with 20 percent of that same element. Just like in baking, the possibilities are endless!

Important alloys to iron:

Carbon

Chromium

Cobalt

Nickel

Manganese

Silicon

Tungsten

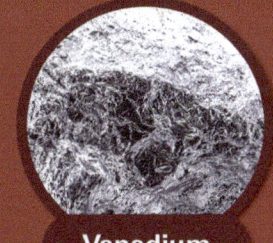
Vanadium

DID YOU KNOW?

When is iron not an element? When it's an alloy! Iron is used as a term for both the chemical element iron and alloys in which iron is the main ingredient. Iron can form alloys with just about any metal element and many nonmetals.

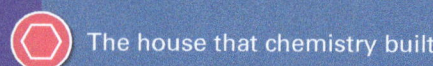
The house that chemistry built

Strong steel

One *alloy* ingredient to iron stands above the rest: carbon. When just a dash of carbon is added in the making of an iron alloy, the resultant product is incredibly strong. Steel is any alloy of iron that contains less than 2 percent carbon. There are many kinds of steel alloys for different applications. They are all incredibly strong, easy to work, and cheap!

Structural steel refers to the kinds of steel used in buildings and other structures. Such alloys have a very low percentage of carbon. Some formulas have additional ingredients, but others are just iron and carbon. Structural steel forms the I-beams, rods, and bolts that hold up so many buildings.

When you think of a strong, tall building, you think of steel. Steel is the material that has allowed buildings to reach incredible heights and cover vast areas.

Structural steel can hold up way more than its own weight. To build skyscrapers, architects design floor after floor of steel platforms sandwiched between steel columns. Each column holds up the weight of all the floors above it, acting like the internal skeleton of the building. In this setup, the walls don't support any weight and serve only to keep out the elements. They're like the skyscraper's skin!

Prior to the development of **steel-frame construction** in the late 1800's, tall buildings were supported by their walls. The walls had to be thick to support the weight of all those stories. Thick walls reduced a building's floorspace, lowering the rent the owners could collect. Around 1900 in Chicago and other places, engineers began strengthening masonry walls with iron and steel beams. It quickly became apparent that skeletons of such beams could support tall buildings entirely on their own.

- The house that chemistry built

Rust busts steel

Nobody wants their car to rust!

The mottled brown blemishes aren't a pretty sight. But rust damage is not just cosmetic. It weakens the metal, in addition to corroding the surface. Long exposure to air and moisture will cause nails to rust off and rust holes to form in sheet iron. In a building, bridge, or other structure, such damage can lead to a catastrophic collapse.

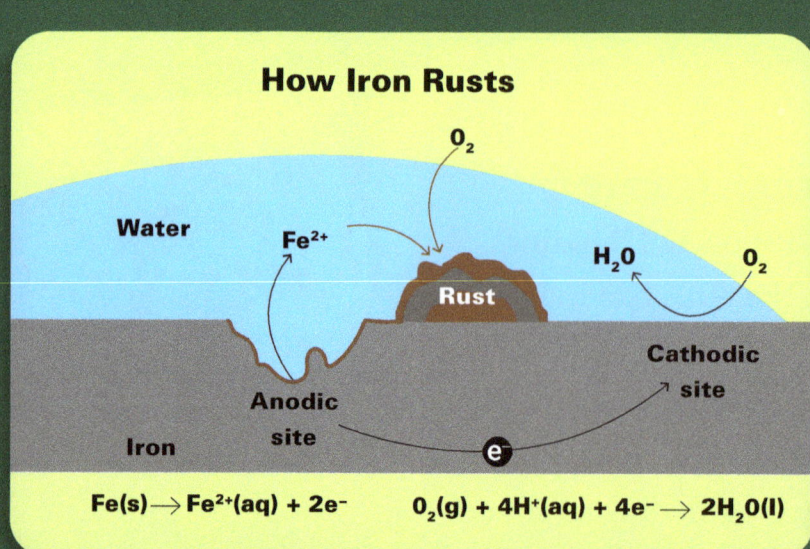

How Iron Rusts

$Fe(s) \rightarrow Fe^{2+}(aq) + 2e^-$

$O_2(g) + 4H^+(aq) + 4e^- \rightarrow 2H_2O(l)$

Rust is formed by the union of the oxygen of the air with the iron in a process called *oxidation*. Oxidation is a chemical reaction in which a substance loses electrons. In the presence of water, iron atoms lose their electrons and become negatively charged *ions* suspended in the water. These ions combine with oxygen and accumulate on the surface as rust.

Iron and steel have one great weakness: rust. *Rust* is a brownish-red substance that forms on the surface of iron or steel when it is exposed to damp air.

Architect of a nation and *a university campus!*

Rust can cause significant damage to iron structures. In 1997, during a graduation ceremony at the University of Virginia, a balcony collapsed, killing 1 person and injuring 18. Investigations revealed the accident was caused by a wrought iron rod that had rusted over the course of 175 years. Because the rod was hidden by wooden paneling, the building inspectors were absolved of blame along with the building's architect—third president of the United States Thomas Jefferson.

Manufacturers can protect exposed iron and steel through *galvanizing*. Galvanizing coats the metal with a thin protective layer of zinc or zinc alloy. The zinc helps prevent corrosion because it reacts with many chemicals more easily than iron does. It reacts with oxygen in the environment to form zinc oxide, preventing the formation of rust.

DID YOU KNOW?

Hey! Who are you calling rusty?!?

Mars is rusty! The Red Planet gets its reddish color from iron oxides on its surface. These are the same compounds that form in rust. Maybe it should be called the Rusty Planet!

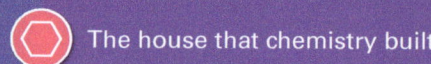

The house that chemistry built

Concrete strength

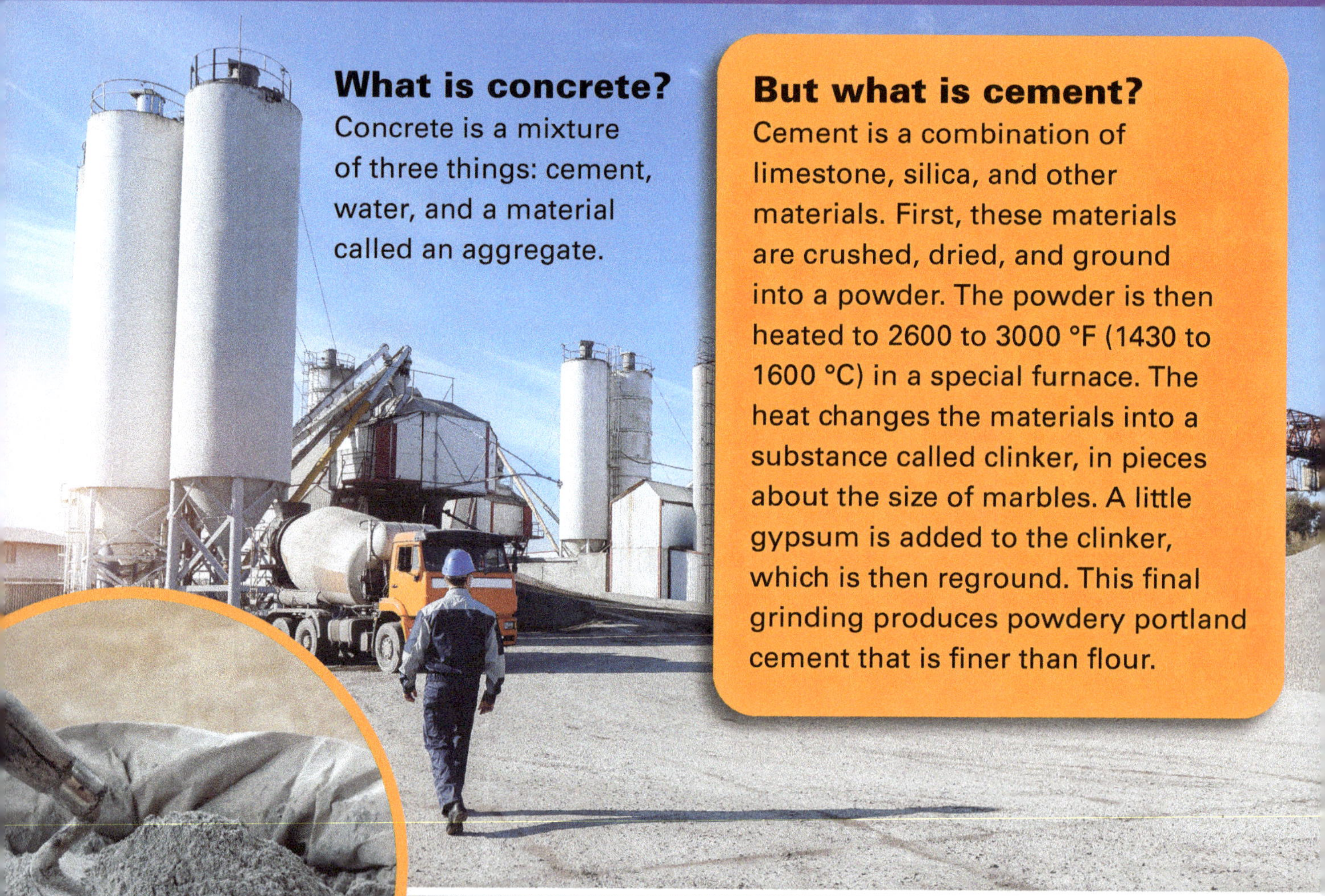

What is concrete?
Concrete is a mixture of three things: cement, water, and a material called an aggregate.

But what is cement?
Cement is a combination of limestone, silica, and other materials. First, these materials are crushed, dried, and ground into a powder. The powder is then heated to 2600 to 3000 °F (1430 to 1600 °C) in a special furnace. The heat changes the materials into a substance called clinker, in pieces about the size of marbles. A little gypsum is added to the clinker, which is then reground. This final grinding produces powdery portland cement that is finer than flour.

Aggregates bulk up the mix and give the cement something to stick to. Aggregates are such materials as sand, gravel, crushed rock, and blast furnace slag (waste). The kind of aggregate included in the mix helps determine the concrete's physical properties after it's poured.

It's hard to top synthetic rock.
Concrete is the foundation—often literally—of modern building construction.

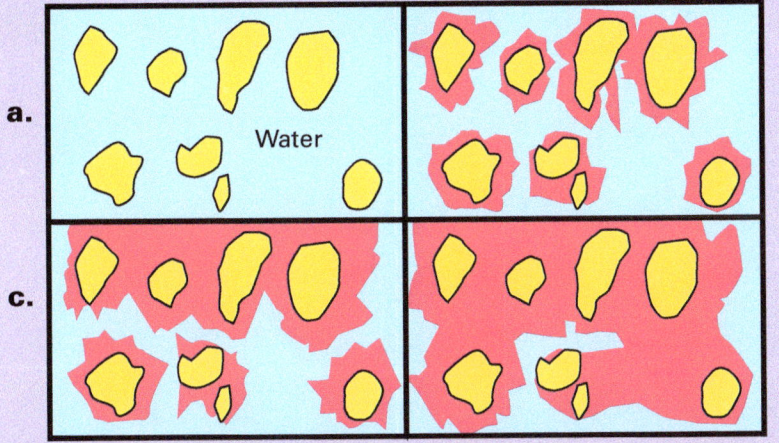

Hydration Reaction Stages

a. Hydration has not occurred; b. Beginning of hydration; c. Hydration continues; d. Nearly hardened cement paste

Water is the secret ingredient that turns powdery cement and chunky aggregates into rock-hard cement. When water is mixed into the cement and aggregate, the materials undergo a series of complex chemical reactions called hydration. In hydration, the disparate pieces form chemical bonds with one another.

Concrete engineers and construction workers make sure to measure the exact quantities of cement, aggregates, and water for the mix of concrete they're working with. If too little or too much of one ingredient is added, the concrete will be too hard to work with or too weak.

DID YOU KNOW?

People might say that concrete "dries," but in fact it *cures*. It turns from liquid to solid, but very little of the water evaporates from it. In fact, workers often spray water onto the surface of curing concrete to replace water lost to evaporation, so the top of the concrete will cure similarly to the bottom.

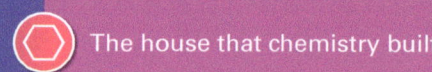

The house that chemistry built

Uses for concrete

Concrete has great compressive strength but little tensile strength. That means it can resist high loads pushing down on it, but it tends to crumble when pulled. Engineers have compensated for this weakness by joining concrete with steel. Long, thin poles of steel, called rebar, are fixed into place in a gridlike layout where the concrete is to be poured. The tensile strength of the steel rods complements the compressive strength of concrete to make reinforced concrete strong in all directions.

A rotary tube furnace is used to produce cement clinker.

Concrete has an extremely high *embodied energy*. Every step of the process takes energy, from mining the ingredients to firing and grinding the clinker, to transporting the finished concrete. All that energy use makes concrete bad for the environment. But, engineers are working to develop greener concrete. Ideas include using local material as the aggregate, using solar energy to power the heating and grinding, and even creating concrete that absorbs carbon dioxide as it cures or serves as a ***catalyst*** to clean toxic smog out of the air! The technology already exists—the real trick is making it cheaper and getting governments on board to help pay for it.

Wherever you are, you're probably not far from concrete.

This amazing material is used everywhere!

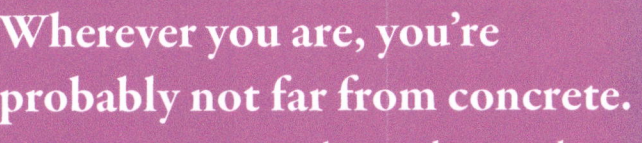

Despite the material's high embodied energy, manufacturers crank out concrete at a colossal clip. Over 170 tons (150 metric tons) of new concrete are produced *each minute!* That's enough to pour a new driveway every 12 seconds!

That's a lot of driveways!

The ancient Romans discovered **concrete** and used it frequently to create impressive buildings and public works. But knowledge of the material was lost following the collapse of the Roman Empire in A.D. 476. The technology wasn't reinvented until the mid-1700's!

The house that chemistry built

Another brick in the wall

Bricks are rectangular building blocks made of clay, shale, or various other materials. Bricks are strong, hard, and resistant to fire and damage from the weather. They are used to build such structures as houses, commercial and public buildings, fireplaces, and furnaces.

Bricks are formed from a material called clay. Clay consists of extremely small particles of rock that measure less than 4 microns, or about 1/10,000 of an inch, in diameter. Clay minerals consist mainly of tiny, sheetlike structures of alumina and silica bound together by other elements.

Water *molecules* interspersed in clay enable the alumina and silica to slide around. This enables clay to be worked and molded into different shapes!

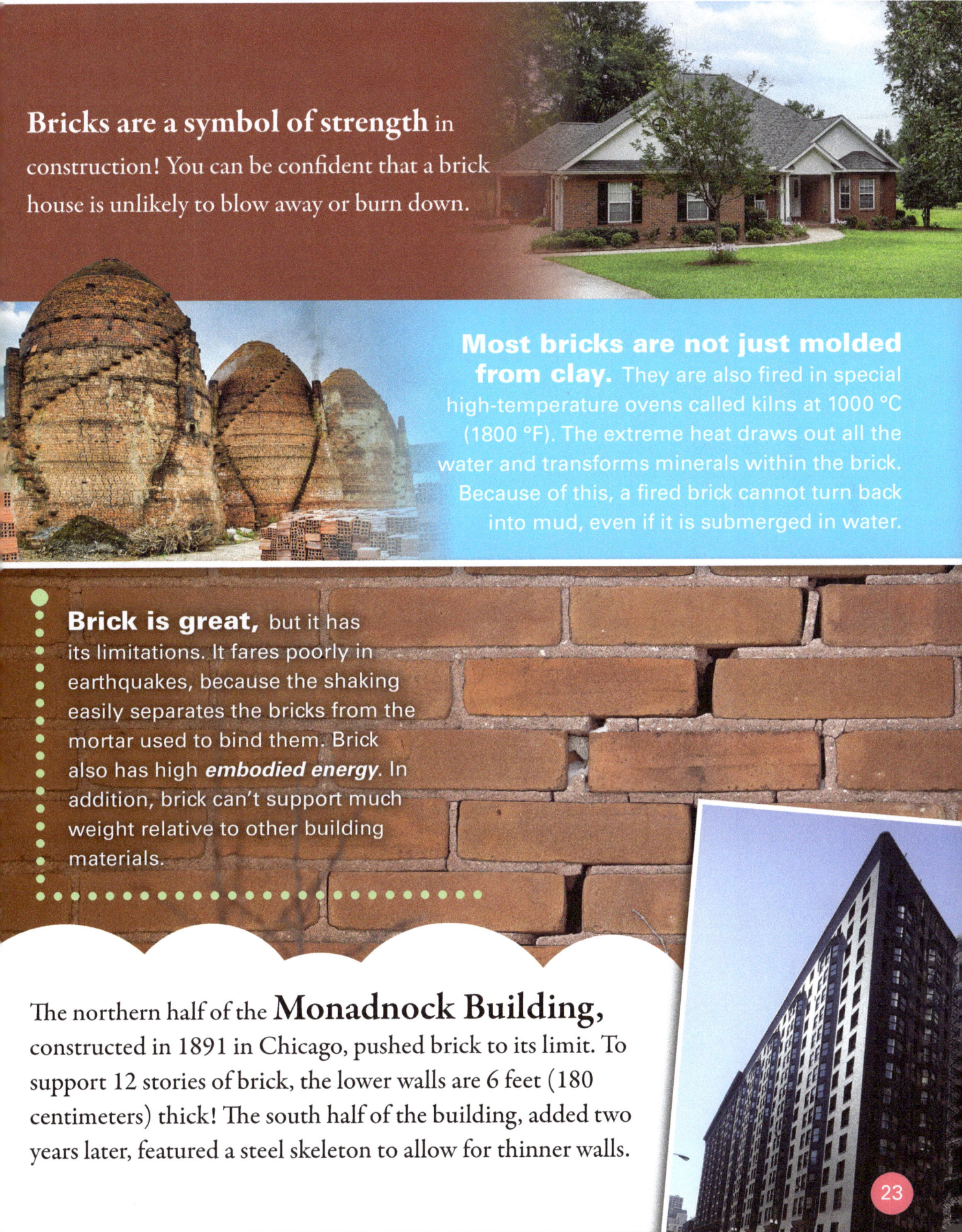

Bricks are a symbol of strength in construction! You can be confident that a brick house is unlikely to blow away or burn down.

Most bricks are not just molded from clay. They are also fired in special high-temperature ovens called kilns at 1000 °C (1800 °F). The extreme heat draws out all the water and transforms minerals within the brick. Because of this, a fired brick cannot turn back into mud, even if it is submerged in water.

Brick is great, but it has its limitations. It fares poorly in earthquakes, because the shaking easily separates the bricks from the mortar used to bind them. Brick also has high *embodied energy*. In addition, brick can't support much weight relative to other building materials.

The northern half of the **Monadnock Building,** constructed in 1891 in Chicago, pushed brick to its limit. To support 12 stories of brick, the lower walls are 6 feet (180 centimeters) thick! The south half of the building, added two years later, featured a steel skeleton to allow for thinner walls.

The house that chemistry built

Mudbrick

The main ingredient in mudbrick, of course, is mud. But how can you make a hard brick out of squishy mud? Mud is consists of very small pieces of rock, including clay, held together with water. Just as with clay, water keeps these particles stuck together, but it also allows them to slide past one another.

To make mudbricks, workers collect clay and other suitable earth and mix it with water and a binding material. This mixture is placed into forms or is worked by hand into bricks. The bricks are then left in the sun for weeks to cure. Curing drives out much of the water, enabling clay particles to form chemical bonds with one another.

Mudbricks defy the high *embodied energy* of other building materials. Clay for making mudbricks can generally be collected at or near the construction site. Local ingredients, such as discarded stalks from farming, can be used as binder. Bricks are usually made by hand, rather than machine. And of course, only the sun's energy is needed to bake them. The result is a building material that can have virtually no embodied energy! Adobe is also totally recyclable. Exposure to rain may be enough to turn a rubbled structure back into mud!

People made bricks for thousands of years before the advent of high-temperature kilns. Instead, they made mudbricks. Mudbrick, also called adobe, isn't merely a building material of the past. It's undergoing a resurgence because it can be environmentally friendly.

But why use adobe as a building material if melts in the rain? Sure, you can't build a mudbrick building underwater, but the bricks are strong enough that a little water isn't going to turn your mudroom into a mud room. Builders using mudbricks coat the structure with special sealers to repel rain and resist temperature changes. Deep eaves can also prevent rainwater from hitting the structure. A solid foundation—and even a few *courses* (layers) of fired bricks at the bottom—help keep damp from leaking into the structure.

Mmm, adobe!

Mudbrick is not without its problems—even beyond moisture concerns. Termites like to burrow into it and eat any organic binding agents inside. Adobe is also not a great insulator, and it tends to crumble in earthquakes. Builders can add various ingredients to improve its performance, but this process raises adobes embodied energy and complicates recycling.

The house that chemistry built

Let the sunshine in

One of the reasons that glass is widely used is because it's so cheap! All its components are available in many places throughout the world. Glass has three main ingredients: silica, calcium carbonate, and limestone. Silica is just a fancy name for sand! It can be collected near the shorelines of oceans and the beds of rivers and lakes. Calcium carbonate can be mined from the ground, refined from certain kinds of plant material, or manufactured. And limestone is found in quarries everywhere!

To make glass, manufacturers first mix precise combinations of the materials. Then, they may add *cullet*. Cullet is either recycled glass or waste glass from a previous melt of the same kind of glass. Adding cullet to the batch uses materials that otherwise would be wasted. It also reduces the amount of heat needed to melt the new batch of raw materials.

The mixture is placed in a furnace, where it's heated to as much as 2900 °F (1600 °C). Window glass is made by pouring the melted mixture onto a pool of molten tin. The glass is lighter than the tin, so it floats. The glass also has a higher melting point than the tin, so it solidifies while the tin stays molten. The solid plates are then removed from the pool of tin to cool further. Glass formed this way is called float glass.

Imagine a force field that keeps out air and solid objects but is practically invisible. Oh—and it does so without using energy. Such a force field exists—it's glass! No building would feel complete without it.

Glass is an amorphous solid. That means it's not a crystal, and there is no specific temperature at which it hardens into a solid structure. For this reason, glass is sometimes called a super-cooled liquid. You might have heard that glass in old buildings has "flowed" over decades or centuries, causing it to be thicker on the bottom than on top. Glass can *theoretically* flow at room temperature, but even the gloopiest glass only flows about 1 nanometer in 1 billion years!

So why *is* the glass of some older windows **thicker at the bottom?** It's due to how they were manufactured. Prior to the invention of the float-glass technique, glass was much harder to make. To make window glass, a glassmaker would take a large blob of melted glass on a glass-blowing pipe and spin it into a flat disk. Workers would cut multiple windowpanes from the disk after it cooled. Because the disk was thicker toward the edges, panes made from it would have a thicker and thinner edge. Builders often naturally oriented the thicker edge toward the ground.

The house that chemistry built

Roofing

Asphalt shingles are the dominant style of roofing for homes in North America. Such shingles begin with a flat base material, usually a fiberglass mat. Fiberglass is glass in the form of fine *fibers* (threads). These are made of the same ingredients as other glass, but the molten material is pushed or pulled through tiny holes to make thin fibers. The fibers may be many times finer than human hair and may look and feel like silk. The flexible glass fibers are stronger than steel, however, and will not burn, stretch, rot, or fade.

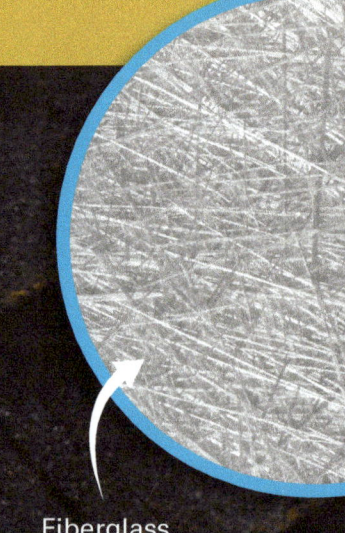

Fiberglass

The mats are then coated in asphalt. Asphalt is a black, cementlike substance that is found in most crude oil. It's the gunk at the bottom after the liquid oil has been drained off! Asphalt consists of long-chain **hydrocarbon molecules**, often with more than 300 atoms bonded together! These long-chain molecules make asphalt *thermoplastic*—that is, asphalt softens and becomes a liquid when heated, because high temperatures make it easier for the chains to slide past one another. Likewise, asphalt returns to a solid when cooled. Asphalt doesn't wear easily and is highly waterproof.

However, asphalt is damaged by ultraviolet (UV) radiation put out by the sun. To protect roofing shingles, manufacturers coat the still-hot asphalt with granules of crushed rock. These granules block UV light and give the shingle its color.

Roofs have a tough job! Wind, rain, hail, and sunshine beat down on a building, and the brunt of the battering is borne by the roof. Therefore, roofing materials have to be tough.

There are plenty of other kinds of roofing, though! Tile roofs are made of clay that is then fired to high temperatures. Just like shingles, the tiles are installed in layered fashion to allow water to run off the roof without collecting at any joints.

Metal roofs are also popular. In historic times, copper paneling covered the tops of important structures, such as city halls and houses of worship. Today, there are all kinds of metal roofs, including aluminum, copper, galvanized steel, and zinc.

2 INSIDE THE HOME

A building isn't finished after the walls go up! Think about all the things that make your home complete: bright walls, comfy carpets, shiny floors, and so much more. As you might have guessed, the chemistries of those things give them the properties that make them useful—and beautiful.

Chemistry is what makes a house a home! Interior finishes get their properties from chemistry, too.

Even the earliest interior decorators used chemistry. Many thousands of years ago, prehistoric peoples across the world **decorated caves** with beautiful, expressive art. The *pigments* (coloring agents) they used include charcoal, manganese, and red ochre. Ancient painters usually mixed one or more of these minerals with a *binder* or *extender*. A binder is a material that helps the paint stick to the cave wall. An extender is a material that artists use along with water to extend pigment and make it easier to apply. Common binder materials include blood, oils, or egg whites. Commonly used extenders include the minerals biotite and feldspar.

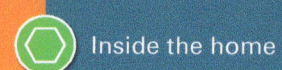
Inside the home

Staying warm with insulation

A roof and walls might protect a home from rain and snow, but typical construction materials allow heat to travel through them easily. Therefore, builders turn to special materials to keep building occupants comfortable. Insulation reduces the flow of heat outward during cold weather and inward during hot weather.

Some insulation materials have chemical makeups that make them resistant to heat transfer. More commonly, however, they contain tiny pockets of air or other gases. These dead air spaces are resistant to heat transfer. The same principle is used in double-glazed windows. Glass readily transfers heat, so a single-paned window lets out a lot of heat in the winter. In a double-glazed window, nitrogen or another *inert* (nonreactive) gas is sealed between two panes of glass. It is much harder for heat to move through this gas.

What good is a building that leaves its occupants sweating in the summer and shivering in the winter? Insulation reduces mechanical heating and air conditioning demands and makes a building more comfortable.

Mineral wool looks like cotton candy—and it's made in a similar way! Rock, glass, or another mineral is melted at temperatures well over 1,000 degrees. A stream of air is forced through the molten mixture, causing solid strands to form as the mixture cools rapidly in the air. These strands are collected and mixed with a binding agent to form thick, fluffy batts. Just don't try to eat them!

Instead of lugging cumbersome batts, you can just spray in insulation! Two groups of chemicals, one called *isocyanate* and one called *polyol*, are sprayed onto a surface. When combined, they react to form solid polyurethane. The expanding foam works its way into crevices and around obstructions. Gas formed in the reaction becomes trapped in the expanding polyurethane. Once hardened, the foam can be cut down to size.

DID YOU KNOW?

Mineral wool is inspired by a process that occurs naturally in volcanoes that spout runny lava. Droplets harden into long strands that float on the breeze. These strands get caught in trees and antennas and cover the ground. The strands are named Pele's hair after the Hawaiian goddess of fire and volcanoes.

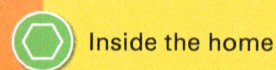
Inside the home

Asbestos: deadly rock fibers

Asbestos is any of a group of soft, threadlike mineral fibers. The mineral group serpentine includes chrysotile, the best known, most abundant, and most widely used type of asbestos. The crystal structure of chrysotile consists of alternating sheets of magnesia and silica. These sheets are rolled into tubes called fibrils that resemble a rolled-up newspaper.

People knew of asbestos for centuries, but it remained mostly a novelty. The material's resistance to fire and heat made it extremely valuable during the Industrial Revolution. The Industrial Revolution was a period in the late 1700's and early 1800's in which great changes took place in the lives and work of people in several parts of the Western world, including an increased reliance on machinery. Asbestos was used to insulate boilers, furnaces, and pipes. It was added to brake pads, cement, bricks, and floor tiles.

34

For centuries, people marveled at the amazing insulating and fireproofing properties of the natural material asbestos. But, people are now aware of its dangers.

Asbestos is not a health hazard as long as it remains in place. People live in homes containing asbestos today. When asbestos is disturbed, however, it fractures and sheds tiny particles. These asbestos particles float in the air and are easily inhaled. Inside the lungs, these fibers damage tissue and cause respiratory diseases.

Eventually, the dark side of the fire-resistant fiber was revealed. Asbestos producers became aware of the health hazards of the material in the 1930's, but they hid the dangers from their employees and fought government regulation. It took many decades for public awareness and regulation to remove asbestos from the myriad products it had found its way into.

Legend has it that the famous European king **Charlemagne** would host lavish dinner parties upon a beautiful white tablecloth. When dinner was over, the king would order the soiled tablecloth to be thrown into the fire. To the astonishment of the dinner guests, the tablecloth would not burn. The tablecloth was made of pure asbestos fibers! The fire would clean the tablecloth so it was ready for the next banquet.

I have all the best party tricks!

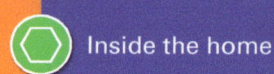

Inside the home

Vital molecule: argon

STATS

Symbol
Ar

Atomic Number
18

Atomic Mass
39.948

Discoverers
Sir William Ramsay; Baron Rayleigh

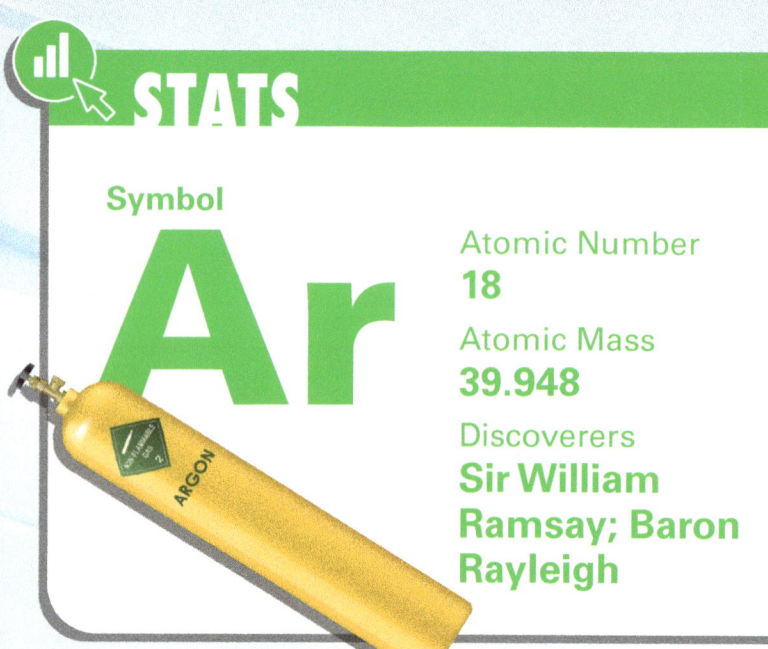

The English physicist Lord Rayleigh and the Scottish chemist Sir William Ramsay discovered argon in 1894. It's fitting that a knight and a baron discovered argon because it's a noble gas! Chemists often divide the elements into classes based on shared properties. Argon's class, the noble gases, rarely react with other elements. Only one argon-containing **compound** is known to exist!

Argon's nonreactivity makes it quite useful. The oxygen in the air can corrode the filaments of incandescent and fluorescent light bulbs. Therefore, manufacturers fill the bulbs with nonreactive argon to greatly extend the bulbs' lifespans.

Lord Rayleigh

Sir William Ramsay

"A noble gas for noble guys!"

Argon is a gas that plays a small but important role in many buildings.

Argon does not conduct heat as well as does air. Filling the space between panes of double-glazed windows with argon super-charges their insulation performance.

In the factory, argon is used as a shielding gas in arc welding. It protects the molten metal from oxygen in the air.

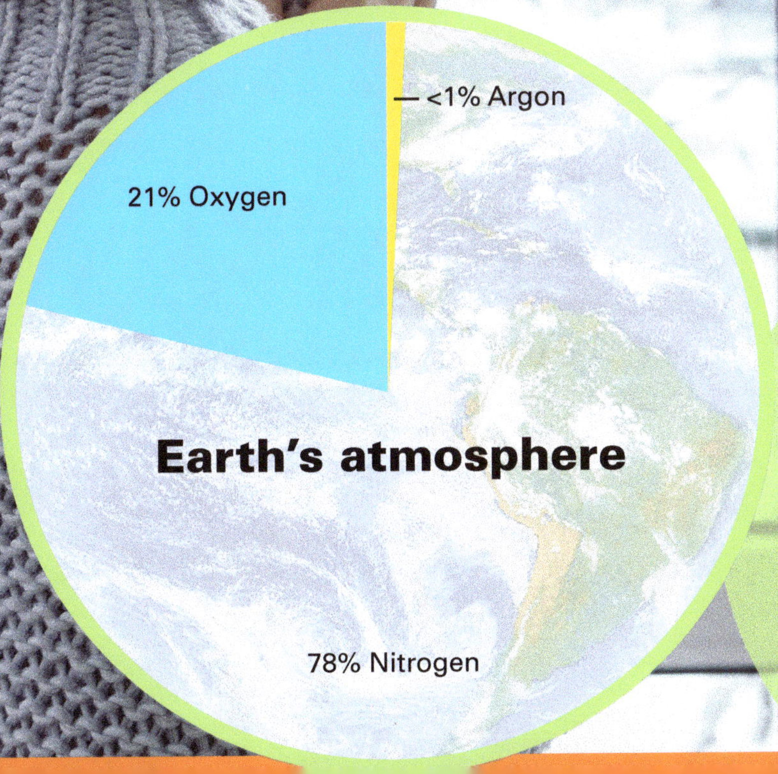

— <1% Argon

21% Oxygen

Earth's atmosphere

78% Nitrogen

DID YOU KNOW?

Argon is the third most common gas in Earth's atmosphere! Nitrogen is first at 78 percent, followed by oxygen at 21 percent.

 Inside the home

Drywall

Drywall is a kind of board made of gypsum and paper. Gypsum is *hydrated* calcium sulfate. Hydrated means that it contains water. Drywall is used to cover such large areas as walls and ceilings. It protects against fire and weather and some insulation against heat and cold. It absorbs sound and also serves a decorative purpose. Think about it: clean, paintable walls look a lot better than a jumble of studs, wires, pipes, and insulation! Drywall is made in sheets $^1/_{10}$ inch to 3 inches (2.5 to 76 millimeters) thick. It is sold in sections up to 8 feet (2.4 meters) wide and 20 feet (6 meters) long.

Despite being a crystal, naturally occurring gypsum is extremely soft and pliable—you can scratch it with a fingernail and bend it with your bare hands! These properties are what make it great for drywall. It's strong enough to form sturdy boards, but those boards can easily be cut to shape and screwed into place.

The part of a wall you can see inside a room likely isn't helping to hold the building up. But it's far from dead weight! Drywall is like a room's skin. It serves many purposes to make a home comfy and cozy.

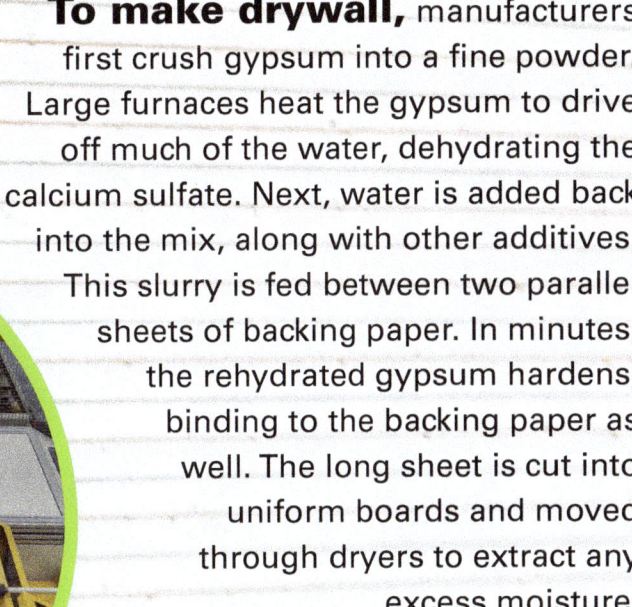

To make drywall, manufacturers first crush gypsum into a fine powder. Large furnaces heat the gypsum to drive off much of the water, dehydrating the calcium sulfate. Next, water is added back into the mix, along with other additives. This slurry is fed between two parallel sheets of backing paper. In minutes, the rehydrated gypsum hardens, binding to the backing paper as well. The long sheet is cut into uniform boards and moved through dryers to extract any excess moisture.

CAREER CORNER

A do-it-yourselfer can tackle drywall, but it takes a lifetime to master. Drywall installers cut, hang, and finish drywall paneling. After installing the boards, they bind the edges with a special tape and cover the edges and screw holes with a mudlike *compound* that dries to form a smooth surface.

Inside the home

Household paint chemistry

Plain drywall may look better than studs and pipes, but it's still pretty dull. Paint protects drywall's surface, covers over any imperfections, and makes it look nicer!

Paint consists of one or more finely ground *pigments* and a liquid *vehicle*. Pigments determine the color of the paint and provide it with certain other properties. Manufacturers often add clay, mica, and talc to paint to increase its resistance to wear. These semitransparent materials are called *extenders* or *inert pigments*. Such pigments as zinc phosphate and barium metaborate help paint to protect metal surfaces against **rust**.

Nothing brightens up a room like a fresh coat of paint. Paints are marvels of chemistry! Today's paint is easier to apply, cleaner looking, and more environmentally friendly than ever before.

There are several different kinds of paint.

You wouldn't want to paint the inside of your house with the same paint that covers a car, for example. Household paint is also called architectural paint. Today household paint is almost always latex paint. Latex paint is now made with special resins, not latex, but the name stuck.

Coalescence

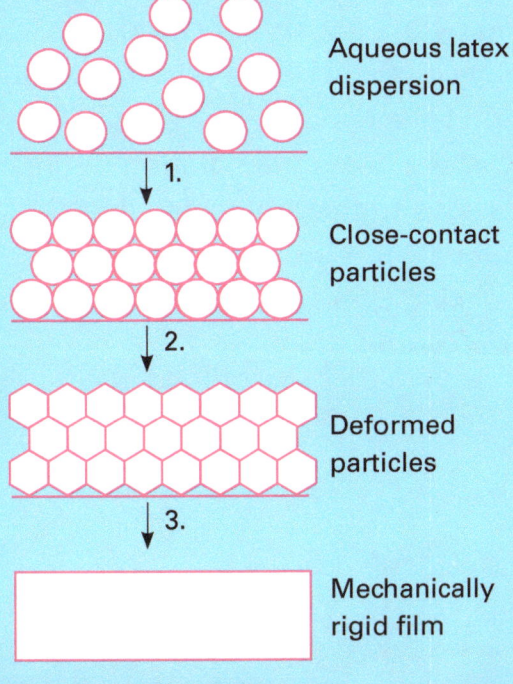

1. Aqueous latex dispersion
2. Close-contact particles
3. Deformed particles

Mechanically rigid film

Watching paint dry might be boring, but there are exciting chemical reactions going on behind the scenes! Latex paints cure by *coalescence*. In this process, the resin molecules bond together to form a dry paint film. This bonding occurs as the water *evaporates* (turns from liquid to gas) from the painted surface.

Lead-based house paint became popular in the early 1900's. **Lead compounds** were found to speed up drying, increase the paint's durability, and make it more resistant to moisture. But as these paints aged, they shed chips and dust, which were later determined to be extremely toxic. Yikes!

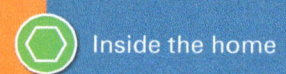

Inside the home

Chemistry will floor you!

Most carpets today are made from stain-resistant synthetic materials, including nylon. Nylon fibers are durable and easy to dye. They consist of large **hydrocarbon** molecules. A solution of nylon salts is put in a machine called an autoclave. The autoclave heats the solution under pressure. The water is removed, and the molecules that make up each of the compounds combine to form very large molecules. This process of making large molecules from smaller ones is called **polymerization**.

Fibers are made by forcing molten nylon through tiny holes in a device called a spinneret. The streams of nylon harden into filaments when they strike the air. These filaments are spun together to make yarn for carpet pile.

From frizzy carpets to sparkling tile, chemistry underlies our homes' floors. It delivers surfaces that resist wear, feel comfy, clean easily, and look beautiful.

Ceramic tiles are another flooring staple. Ceramic is also used on the walls of kitchens and bathrooms because of its water resistance and easy cleaning. Ceramic tiles are created in much the same way as bricks. But before entering the kiln, most tiles are sprayed with a glaze. The glaze bonds to the surface of the tile in the heat of the kiln. It makes the tile resistant to water and stains—and gives it color, too!

CAREER CORNER

Which type of floor should you pick for your space? How will it match the rest of the room? If you love answering questions like this, you could be an interior designer! Interior designers create rooms and other indoor areas that are attractive, comfortable, and useful. Interior design involves the careful selection of items to suit the purpose and overall mood of an area. It's not just for homes, either. Professional interior designers also plan and create interiors for hotels, hospitals, libraries, office buildings, schools, and stores—even the interiors of airplanes and automobiles!

Material strength

What you'll need:
- Materials to test, such as:
  1. A small wooden food skewer or popsicle stick
  2. A disposable plastic utensil
  3. A plastic straw
  4. A crayon
  5. A rolled-up paper tube
- Thread or yarn
- A very small basket (You might have to make one yourself out of construction paper!)
- A weight set or a bunch of coins or batteries
- Safety glasses

Give it a try
1. For each material to be tested, tie the thread and basket at the very end of the piece.
2. Hold the piece at the edge of the table, with about 2 inches (5 centimeters) sticking out.
3. Can the material hold the basket without breaking? Mark down your results.
4. Now, add weights to the basket one by one. Note whether the material bends before breaking. Mark down how many weights the material could hold (one less than the number at which it broke).

Chemistry gives different materials different strengths. Let's test different materials to see which can better resist a load!

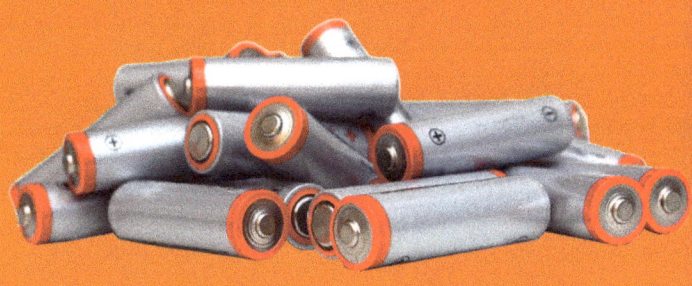

Materials	Material hold? Yes or no	How many weights material can hold
Small wooden food skewer or popsicle stick		
Plastic utensil		
Plastic straw		
Crayon		
Rolled-up paper tube		

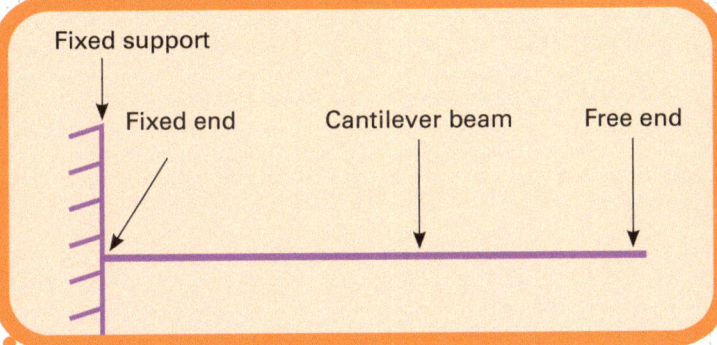

Try this next!

In this test, your materials were cantilevers. A cantilever is a beam that is supported at one end only. Loading up your cantilevers subjected them to *shear stress*. Can you set up a way to test the materials for other kinds of mechanical stress, such as compression, torsion, or tension?

QUESTION TIME!

Which of your materials was the strongest? Do engineers and architects design buildings or other structures with these materials? Why or why not? Could they?

Index

A
alloys, 12-14, 17
architecture (career), 7
argon, 36-37
asbestos, 34-35
asphalt, 28
atoms, 12, 16, 28, 36-37

B
blood, 12-13, 31
bricks, 22-25, 34

C
cantilevers, 45
carbon, 9, 13-14
carbon dioxide, 9, 12, 20
catalysts, 20
cave paintings, 31
cells, of wood, 8
cellulose, 8-9
cement, 18-19, 34
Charlemagne, 35
clay, 22, 24, 29, 40
clinker, 18-20
combustion, 9
compounds, 17, 36, 39, 41-42
concrete, 18-21
copper, 29

D
drywall, 38-40

E
embodied energy, 20-21, 23-25
evaporation, 19, 41

F
fiberglass, 28
fighter planes, 10
fire, 9, 11, 22, 35

G
galvanizing, 17, 29
glass, 26-28, 32-33
gypsum, 18, 38-39

H
hemicellulose, 8
hemoglobin, 12
hydrocarbons, 28, 42

I
Industrial Revolution, 34
insulation, 32-35, 37-38
interior design (career), 43
ions, 16
iron, 12-17

J
Jefferson, Thomas, 17

L
lead, 41
lignin, 8-9
limestone, 18, 26
lumber, 9-10

M
Mars, 17
mass timber, 11
mineral wool, 33
molecules, 12, 22, 28, 36-37, 41-42
Monadnock Building (Chicago), 23
mudbricks, 24-25

N
nitrogen, 32, 37

O
oxidation, 16
oxygen, 9, 12, 16-17, 36-37

P
paint, 31, 40-41
polymerization, 42

R
Ramsay, Sir William, 36
Rayleigh, Lord, 36
rebar, 20
resins, 10-11, 41
Rome, ancient, 21
rust, 16-17, 40

S
silica, 18, 22, 26, 34
steel, 5, 12, 14-17, 20, 23, 29

T
termites, 25
thermoplasticity, 28

U
ultraviolet (UV) radiation, 28

W
water, 9, 16, 18-19, 22-24, 29, 31, 38-39, 41
wood, 8-11

Z
zinc, 17, 29, 40

Glossary

alloy (AL oy)—a mixture of a metal and at least one other element

atom (AT uhm)—one of the most basic units of matter, consisting of a nucleus (core) of particles called protons and neutrons with tiny particles called electrons moving around the nucleus

catalyst (KAT uh lihst)—a substance that speeds up chemical reactions

combustion (kuhm BUHS chuhn)—a chemical reaction that gives off heat and light. Combustion involves the rapid combination of oxygen with a fuel to produce burning.

compound (KOM pownd)—a substance that contains more than one kind of atom

embodied energy (ehm BOD eed EHN uhr jee)—the total amount of energy required to make a product or carry out an activity

galvanizing (GAL vuh nyz ing)—the process of coating such metals as iron and steel with a thin protective layer of zinc or zinc alloy. This layer protects the metals from corrosion (chemical damage).

hydrocarbon (HY droh KAHR buhn)—a chemical compound containing hydrogen and oxygen

ion (EYE uhn)—an atom or molecule that has an electric charge

mass timber (mas TIHM buhr)—a building material made up of multiple units of wood joined together with adhesive, dowels, nails, screws, or other fasteners

molecule (MOL uh kyool)—the smallest particle into which a substance can be divided and still have the chemical identity of the original substance

oxidation (OK suh DAY shuhn)—any chemical process in which a substance combines with oxygen

polymerization (POL ih muhr uh ZAY shuhn)—a chemical process in which many small molecules called monomers combine to build much larger molecules called polymers

rust (ruhst)—a brownish-red substance that forms on the surface of iron or steel when it is exposed to damp air

thermoplastic (THUR moh PLAS tihk)—becoming soft and capable of being molded when heated

www.ingramcontent.com/pod-product-compliance
Lightning Source LLC
Chambersburg PA
CBHW061255170426
43191CB00041B/2429